Ata Khasaf Alsady is a Dutch citizen. He holds a Ph.D. in Semiotics from University of Bologna-Italy. A resident of London since 2003, he also studied music in London. He published a book, *Birds: Sketches From Birding,* in 2023 with Austin Macauley Publishers.

Ata Khasaf Alsady
Illustrated by Caterina Spada

TREENESS

Beauty of Round Loneliness and Oneness

Illustrated by Caterina Spada

A CIP catalogue record for this title is available from the British Library.

ISBN 9781035876853 (Paperback)
ISBN 9781035876860 (ePub e-book)

www.austinmacauley.com

First Published 2025
Austin Macauley Publishers Ltd®
1 Canada Square
Canary Wharf
London
E14 5AA

This book is dedicated to the free, playful spirit of the great nature mystic and Zen master, poet, and friend of trees, Taigu Ryokwan (1758-1831).

My sincere appreciation and thank go to many friends who by their comments, suggestions and information have given me to improve the book. I am very grateful for their helpful assistance. I would like to thank in particular: Daniele Barbieri, Caterina Spada, Salvatore Schembari, Queen Nahla, Jessica Morphy, Sherril Mattan-Stuart, Kew Herbarium and Library, Rare Books and Music, the British Library, and the National Poetry Library, London. To all I say: Thank you for your kindness in supporting me in everything.

Prelude to the Mighty Tree

We are trying our utmost to understand the hidden aspects of the Tree and to reveal its secrets, and find not the outward appearance of the Tree, but to touch its very heart. The Tree is one of the creative and artistic spirits of nature, and it cannot exist without the sun, light, rain and soil. It cannot exist without a Treeness (the essence), which is its spiritual quality.

If it had not been a spirit, there would be no splitting buds, no blooming flowers. It is like the spirit of energy of heaven, earth and nature. If there were no spirit which is beyond the realm of corporeality, there would be no thunder, no lightning, no showers, no sweeping winds.

Trees have also been said to represent physical and spiritual nutrition, fertility, union and liberation. The tree symbol of transcendental aloofness is in the middle of multiplicity and has feelings and emotions, has a heart and a soul, it is not only a shell. And nature without a tree is a body without a soul.

In all of nature, only the tree, for symbolic reasons, is upright like man. The tree is an ever-present model of heroic uprightness. The rounded tree which is turned towards everything is an aerial being living a vertical life high in the sky.

From the tree, we learn the aesthetic of primitive simplicity of nature. The tree lives a solitary and inwardly life detached from the rest, free from materiality and possession, free from murky confusion, free from grasped and grasping. It is most excellently pure and, in its nature, indestructible, and retains its eternal oneness.

Tree has its individual thinking so similar to that of human beings, and it has a way of expressing itself as human beings. Its ideal is to come closer to nature and it is like nature always in motion, never at a standstill as it looks. It is the largest living organism on the planet and has lived more than 1,000 years.

It is round and at the centre of the surroundings and turns like a merry-go-round looking for light. It has a magic aspect: it takes carbon dioxide into its leaves and produces the oxygen we need to breathe. Not knowing the meaning of the Tree is not knowing the mind of nature. Our writings do not express ideas but they put forward images reflecting intuitions.

And those images are immediate expressions of the experience with the trees. So let us go to our Mother Nature and sing of Tree to make life more meaningful and humanity more intensive. Humanity is a part of the natural world, not outside it, not estranged from it.

Let us destroy all artificial barriers we put up between Tree and ourselves, for it is only when they are removed that we can see into the living heart of Tree and love it. And let us also travel on a spiritual journey through the interior of the Tree and its connection between heaven and earth as it carries greenness to the open sky and breathes the free air with the breath of the trees.

We never lose when mystically contemplating the Tree. The tree is the child of nature, nurtured on the bosom of Mother Earth. It is the best friend and master of the heart in pagan nature that offers inspiration and beauty to all. If land is left untended long enough it will eventually become colonised by trees. The happiest man is he who learns from the tree the lesson of worshipping life and nature as real gods.

A tree is a wonderful living organism, it even gives shade to those who wield an axe to cut it down.

Buddha

Split the tree and you will find me.

Jesus Christ

Be like a tree and let the dead leaves drop.

Rumi (1207–1273)

From the pine tree, learn of the pine tree.
And from the bamboo, of the bamboo.

Basho (1644–94)

I read and sing and wish I were a tree.
For sure that I should grow to fruit or shade.

Herbert (Affliction)

Trees are poems that earth writes upon the sky,
We fell them down and turn them into paper,
that we may record our emptiness.

Khalil Gibran

Tree always in the centre
Of all that surrounds it,
Tree feasting upon
Heaven's great dome.

R. M. Rilke

1

Beauty of round loneliness and oneness…
Saint Tree of fantasy
Keeper of its own secrets
That understands the book of the rose.
And read every single leaf.
Red Earth mould clay
Like the handsome Adam
Gently swaying in the breeze
Wine of meditative experiences
Temple of quietude
And eternal aloneness
That thinks in the heart,
And roots.

2

Winds of love…
Oh! Azure breeze
Messenger of relief
Bring me a pleasant whiff.
From the green bark
Of my adored and beloved tree
Pure beyond all kind
Of belief
And creed.

3

Sleeping beauty…
Tall tree of birds
With a sweet windy tune
Lulling the flowers to sleep
In the evening dusk.

4

On its own…
Pure spirit
With beautiful illumination,
Tree of joy
Bountiful beauty
Standing round and upright
With opened buds
Dancing boughs
And blossoming roses,
To greet all
Good and bad
Beautiful and ugly
Happy and sad
And sings:
"Come over here
Sit alongside,
Feel my breath
Listen to every pulse
Beating through my veins,
And be one like me
With Mother Nature."

5

Earthly motherhood…
The tree and I
Are the same wonders of Mother Nature
We look carefully to each other
As we were in a vivid dream
That last forever.

I wish when I die
To be buried next a tree,
So, all my worldly sins
And my too much mundane troubles
Which are on the increase,
Could be washed thoroughly
And purified by the scent
Of its pure and primordial fragrance
That existed before we came to appear.

I heartily worship the tree and praise it,
As a pagan roundness standing Lord
Without dogmas and sacred phantoms books
Dressed all in green with envy,
What a dreamlike sincere one
I call it my supreme God.

6

Dynamic imagination…
A tropical tree
Detaches itself from the worries
Of the day,
Abandons its terrestrial prison,
Becomes a butterfly in spirit
And moves in the wandering wind
From flower to another flower,
To tell the loving intimate secrets
To show the bright moon
The warm night of lovers
And the holy greenness canon,
To rise to where one can live
In a purer realm forever.

7

Sacred white oak tree…
Symbol of strength courage and wisdom
As well as stability,
With inner compass
Withstands strong storms,
Its trunk rises tall and proud
Branching out into a canopy of leaves,
Shelter to all things below
And stillness runs deep
In all interior movements.

Waiting in its illuminated solitude
The sun of Mother Nature,
And its supreme bright light
To descend like a certitude
To let more light in the forest
And to thrive itself.

It is folded by a frozen spirit,
By the coolness of the memory,
Close to the river's water
And to the heart's bounds,
Embraces the birds and the sky together,

Often attacked by ashes of the dread anxiety
And fierce storms
But it is not scared at all.
Its fresh acorns
Are so excited and shakily scare,
Falling of a single leaf
Two leaves and more,
Falling the sweet acorns
But the roots push the sap
To the branches of the soul
Push the dreams to the tree.

Awakened unique Tree
Thirsty to be free from the ardent desires,
And escaping from suffering
Of loneliness and darkness,
With huge resistance and firmness
Furnishing with great accuracy
Its own beloved leaves below
And gazes at the sun's rays
That descends like a love,
Like a sweet water
To embrace like an angel
The heart of the Tree.

8

Waltz of separation…
A dead foliage drifts
Far from its mother tree
Wherever the wind leads,
Has nowhere to go
No goal to achieve,
It does not resist
It does not fight
It just moves everywhere
And nothing is rejected,
Moving without mind
That is the way
Of a poor and humble foliage,
Weeping over this parting
Coldness of leaving
A beloved one behind.

9

Naked solitude…
God asleep in a tree
As twins blended in one,
Free from the web of delusion
In the middle of the world's turmoil,
And to its inner ear speaks
Of simplicity purity and beauty,
Tree soul hears and remembers,
While it is bathing in the sunlight
Of the holy spirit
Unseen by anyone
Save the eye of the soul.

10

Nature miracle…
A small seed
Becomes in its wandering;
A pathway for the stars
And nests for birds
The beech tree.

11

Infinite grace…
Water from a well
Runs towards a thirsty tree,
Proud roots supported the Earth, absorb
And abstract branches
Are intoxicated by joy
And flourishing life.

12

Gospel of Quietism…
Lonely tree
Standing in
A withered field,
Without leaves and bark
In a deep sleep
And green dreams,
Under full moon beams
Has custody of a nest,
Proudly raised towards the sky
What a treeness bless!

13

Tree is pregnant with nature,
The buds are the midwife
The boughs are its tongue and ears,
When it is silent
And calm
Dressed all in green.

14

Primitive simplicity…
I am a pagan tree, like
The sun, water and wind,
And I give myself
To whatever come
To meet me,
I am free
With no prejudice,
I am a real Tree
Little pretty child of Mother Nature.

15

Lost Garden of Eden…
Trees were instruments
In the hands of the unknown Lord,
Free from thoughts and emotions
Like happy bubbles,
Enjoy a state of innocence
And not longing for anything,
But the native fluidity
Perishes at all,
When God uttered:
'Let there be light.'
Then the existential cracks
Begin to show
And grow.

16

Buddha tree…
The sunset
Over the ruins,
Shaded by heart-shaped leaves,
It is still
Its spirit at last free
Evils dissipate
In the morning light,
Such is the battle of the self
That does not take
A form.

17

Pandemic Lockdown…
Just a lonely tree
With a curved shadow
At the bus stop,
And a cat
With a tail forming
A question mark.

18

First living thing…
Creator of life
Old as the world
Magic as a lampstand,
Round at the centre of Eden
Where everything starts,
Tears of joy
Became fruits of the tree.

19

Sunny day…
Tree falls in love,
Birds of paradise
With striking colours,
And bright plumage
Circle around,
And flowers dance
In the breeze,
What a bright and
Cheerful sunny day.

20

Troubled world…
Young leaves lie scattered
Everywhere
Under a crescent moon,
Each under its tree
Waiting for a new dawn
To soon arrive.

21

Going to meet a friend…
This evening,
Alone I hug
And talk to a tree,
Birds' silence
Over my head
Facing the sunset.

22

Light worshipper…
It is because
Of the unmoving thick clouds,
That is why
Its leaves are dry
And seem to cry,
What a fate, knocking
On the tree's trunk!

23

Midsummer's night
Trees speak in whispers
To each other:
'Love is deep
And the path is too long, my dear.'

24

Holly tree…
I am always being here,
And the rain
Softly falls,
While my unsteady leaves
Each one spreads
Rumours and smears I hear,
Against my beloved guests
The emigrated poor birds
Without fixed abode.

25

Something to be proud of…
Out beyond the idea
Of wrongdoing
And right doing,
A misanthropic withered tree
In the middle of a deserted field,
Proudly and cheerful
Lifting a golden cup
Of robin's nest
To the sky,
Chin-chin
I am feeling good
And free
What a wonderful world!

26

Priest of love…
By the river shallows
A solitary tree
In search of something,
It seems to long
For a true treeful companion
And faithful lover
That last forever,
Here there and wherever.

27

Splendid isolation…
A tree
Cannot walk,
But its green spirit
Friend of four seasons,
That grows in itself
And grasps life from within
And from without,
Comes like water
And goes like wind.

28

Heartily constant vigilance…
Flock of birds
In a deep sleep
But the tree is not.

29

Nocturnal scene…
On a quiet tree
Nothing more extraordinary,
Two pretty butterflies
Locked in love
And deep affection,
Ah! What a sincere love
In the air!

30

Keep going on…
In happiness,
In sadness,
The ants are marching
On the tree
Straight ahead!

Tree smiles for them
And welcomes all.

31

Finally,
The bright moon and I
Arrived to the tree
At the same time,
For a trio greenness meeting
In a wild place
Of nowhere.

32

Be or not to be…
Under an oak tree
A man in conversation,
With few wildflowers
Strangled by the wind,
Waiting for a divine salvation
To descend soon
And save them.

33

A splendid torment…
Tired of being tired,
Always there
Dwelling in the same place
Day and night,
The tree of my little garden.

34

Romantic tree…
Every night,
Gazes at the moon
Alone,
With the alone
Humming heartily tune,
By shaking harmoniously
Its leaves.

35

A disciple young branch
Ask the master tree:
What love can you give me?
I give you a green life,
And smugly smiles,
And flourishing healthy life.

36

Redeem…
Morning and evening
I come alone to see,
A solitary round walnut tree.
As a frequent visitor
Poor in spirit,
As a nature lover
And regular worshipper,
To hug and embrace it to my chest.
In the loving calm of its branches
And flourishing fat leaves,
I speak intimately to it
About my inherent sins,
In an impermanent existence
Where every step I take
Is my home,
Is a new story.
Engulfed with anxiety and annihilation
And about my own way,
To find salvation
And gradual purification
Across a bridge of dreams
That floats in brief spring day.

37

An early summer scene…
On the mountain monastery tree
Lands and sleeps
A little white butterfly,
Oh! Goodnight my sweet
You welcome here
Stay with me.
Said the maple tree.

38

The I is forgotten…
Yesterday,
In a green dream,
An old tree accompanied
By all its branches and leaves
Came and knocked on my door.
"*Who is there*," I asked,
"*I am you*," the answer.
I opened the door
Come on
In the house of Oneness

39

Blessed are the poor in spirit…
Somewhere,
A still tree
Half in love
And half in hope,
Serenading loneliness
In the backyard of its soul,
Through deep meditation
And inner harmony.

40

A tall tree
Shrouded in mist,
Gazing over
The grass
And calling,
Why there is no moon
Tonight,
Oh, my loneliness!

41

Seek and follow the evidence…
Very dark clouds
Floating in the river,
Without goal and destination,
Sad tree has just lost
Its sacred God,
The Sun,
That destroys the darkness
Of delusion.

42

Total eclipse…
Looking back
At the summer fire,
No more trees in the fields
Only bewildered birds
Crying:
Home, home, home!

43

Homelessness…
A tree
With a wide heart
That embraces all,
Born of a dream
That sees all mankind,
Come and go,
Longing
For long and strong legs
Of its own,
And walking the path
In the vast forest.

44

Greenness sermon…
An old tree,
Wakes up every morning
By the spiritual sound of the wind
And birds' songs,
To preach various fragrances
And collective wisdom of
The Sacred Treeness Book.
To whom with a third
Inner ear.

45

A tree stuck in the mud,
Listening to the sound of its sigh
And sinking too long,
Into lonely thought
And deep meditation.

46

Tree loneliness…
All by myself
I still exist,
Day and night
No talking
No thoughts
No affects
And an overwhelming sense of loss.
Like an old scarecrow
Standing in the middle of
A wild field,
As a guardian of the place,
As a lighthouse and a shelter
For the lost.

47

Silent witness…
Is the tree,
Knows that many of
Its admired visitors
Are moved to the other world,
Or not yet!
Who knows?

48

In the summer midnight
A tossing and humming tree
In the wind,
Lulling a whole village
To sweetly sleep,
And forget all the worries
Of this transient world
And its troubles.

49

Apostle of poverty and solitude…
Young disciples' leaves ask:
"How do you count us, Guru Tree?"
"With my soul"
Answered the holy Tree,
And smile to all.

50

To be in peace and quiet…
Mother caring tree,
Counts its leaves.
Even at midnight
Before going to sleep.

51

Meeting on the waters…
An enlightened tree,
Turns itself into a prophet
With no ego, dogma and sacred book.
But the power of concentration.
Undergoes a spiritual coup d'etat
In a mental revolution.
Freed from consciousness,
Cleared from all useless things
All around.
Stands all by itself,
And walks on the sacred water,
As if it were the Earth
Hallelujah!

52

Autumn of love…
Lies down
Feeling utterly exhausted,
With broken branches
And broken heart,
A young crooked tree.

53

All dream but not equally…
Feeling very homesick
Aloof giant tree,
Dreams to have fully developed
With two flapping wings.
To go back to heaven.
Its safely sweet eternal abode
To be freed from the sufferings
Of this polluted world.

54

Thick Baobab tree:
I also sleep,
But my dreams
Wait outside
For something that
Has to appear,
From the unknown suchness,
That pays a visit to my mind,
Every night.

55

Light in light…
Solar wanderers in the woods
And worshipers of the light,
Asked the birds,
To urge the Tree
To finish writing its
Book of the light.

56

Deep affection…
Emotional tree
Can’t help falling in love,
With a wild horse,
Galloping everyday
Across the draught fields
With hoofs print of heart-free,
On its way
Broken-hearted,
Every time cries out with pain,
And gentle swell of love
Wishes to gallop also,
And follow him
Wherever goes.

57

A splendid first-class treeness concerto…
Sheets music
Hanging on the branches,
Choir of birds
Softly Sing,
And master Tree
Proudly conducts,
The Green Pastoral Symphony
In the open fresh air
What a joyful scene!

58

Dreamland…
On a cloudy day
I saw my pretty tree,
Close to tears,
Running for fear,
Flowers that worship it also flee
With a pain that more than
They could bear,
I kindly asked it
Why you are running my friend?
Ghastly of nightmare
I hear by my inner ear,
Of voices so near
To cut me for only
A tree sugar shear.

59

Cyclone…
Eradicated young tree
From its roots,
Floats helplessly
In an agitated sea,
No stability,
No flowers in bloom,
And colourful leaves can see
No audacious steering
Over the turbulent waves,
With a solitary bird on it,
Listening to the pattering
Of the rain that
Never ends.

60

Nostalgic Aboriginal breath…
From a hollow trunk
My Didgeridoo is made,
Now plays and speaks
A river of holy sounds,
Freed from everything
Clings to nothing,
It is a depicted spirit
Of a naked tree,
That is blowing
In the air
Of an open sky,
And gently crooning
For something none existent,
To heal the wandering souls
Accompanied by a flowing love,
Like a fountain.

61

Happy birthday Tree Arbol de Tule…*(2)*
I would fit out a ship,
And I would set sail
With an orchestra aboard,
To see it
I will shake its branches,
And kiss its leaves,
And say:
"I wish I'd done
Everything on Earth
With you"
And I would sing
To praise and celebrate
It's happy birthday.

62

Creeping grass
Close to the tree,
Become many
But remain one.
How cool it is!

63

Tree's disquietude…
I think of the past
When I used to stay quiet,
And in lasting peace,
I even myself do not know,
Who the self is?
I just stand strong,
Not by my fruits or branches
But by my imagination,
By the power of my reveries,
And the depth of my roots,
No more asking is needed,
For what service can they ask for,
But now I am surrounded by
Too many sneers,
And parasitic ugly weeds,
Growing where they are
Not wanted at all.
How to get rid of this nightmare?

64

Romance…
At night,
Under a tropical moon,
Two palm trees,
Two faithful lovers,
In a moment of bright love
Branches get entangled,
Leaves shaking with joy,
Bird’s box
Emits huge cries
Of great joy,
For this sincere and intense
Wild and new love,
In the middle of a tropical forest.

65

Thoughtfulness…
The snow of thinking
Covers the tree,
And touches it
With a white thought,
Racing through the mind.

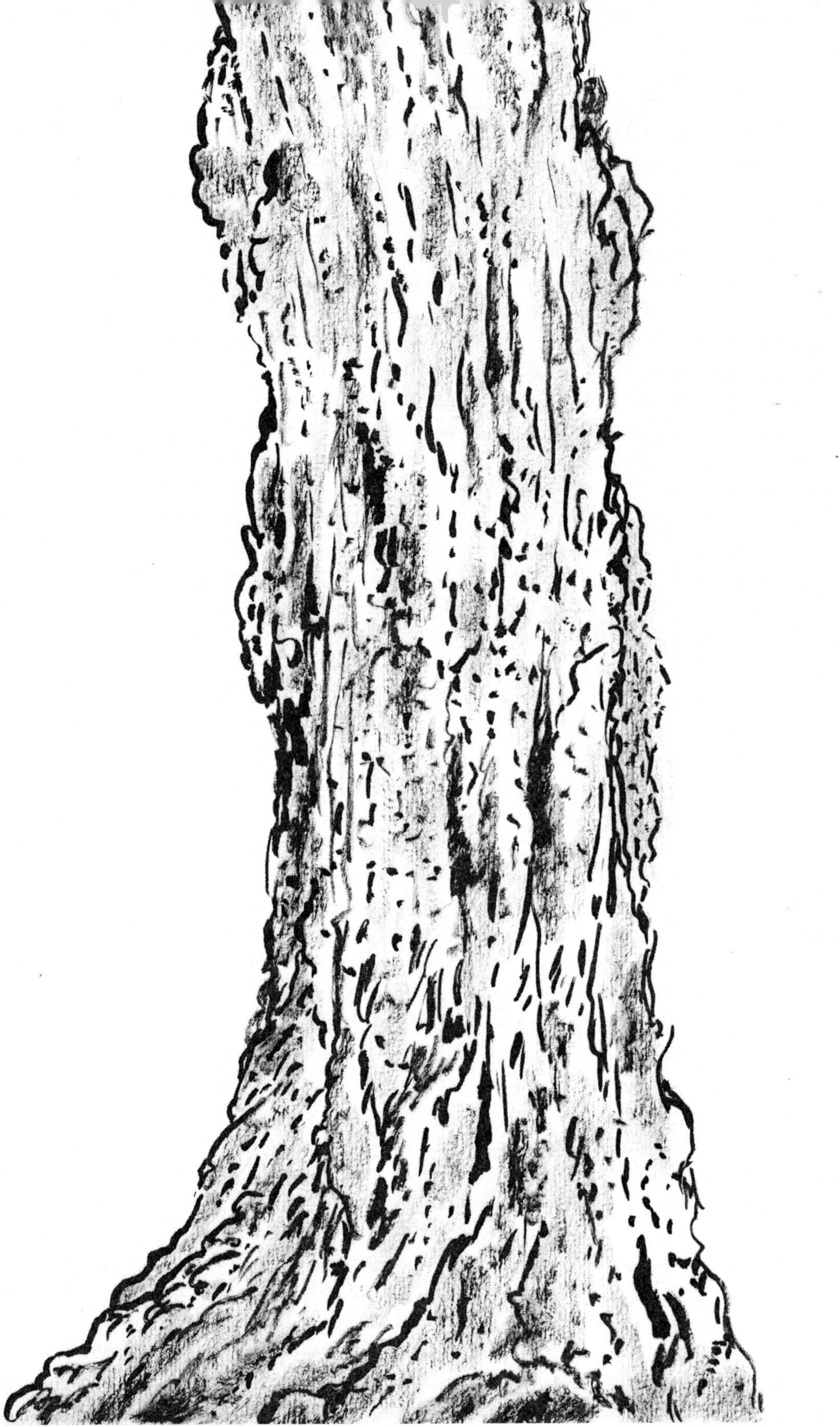

66

Dreamlike desire…
An ash tree
Reflected in the swamp,
In front of me,
I see every day.
With large leaves rustling
As are innumerable wings,
Ready to fly
And be carried off
In the wind,
Like little clouds disappearing
In the heights.

67

First love is a revolution…
Young trees fall in love,
Two souls but with
A single thought,
Two hearts that beat as one,
Branches and leaves kiss
And hold together
In a warm embrace,
Plants spring and bloom
Wind blows,
And migratory birds
Sing for this crazy and beautiful,
Wild treeness love story.

68

Solemn ritual…
In deep stillness,
Where nothing is everything,
Its roots coming out
Breathe fresh air
Mind is free,
Listens to the rain
Dripping from the caves,
The drops become
One with it,
Trees in deep meditation,
In the midst of a remote
Mountain's village.

69

Roaring wind…
Long fleeting shadow of tree
Pointing toward
An untrodden narrow path,
Darkness,
Solitude,
Isolation,
Yet trees whisper to me:
"Friend and dear
You have nothing to fear,
Sooner or later
A light will appear,
And everything will be all right,
Clear and bright."

70

Within walking distance…
Two trees calling,
Each, with a different song,
Sun and moon
In the field,
They enjoy!

71

To be Tree or not to be…
Green leaves,
Asked Mother Tree
Of unknown field,
Which one of us
Will be dropped first
And disappear,
From the existence scene
Of this funny short-life comedy,
For good.

72

Interconnection…
Coast redwood tree
Becomes a long canoe,
And floating gently
Up and down the river,
To bring together
Separated lovers.
What a wonder!

73

Love in the air…
Young tree,
To another tree
Shaking its trunk,
Accompanied by a sweet declaration:
"I am sentimental too."

74

The tormented tree…
Bleeding and weeping
On the mountain,
Whipped by the winds,
Bending under the force
Of a fierce storm,
Shaking and moving
As it were being pulled by hand
That wanted to uproot it.
Nothing tranquil,
No brush can paint it,
No colour can express it
Nothing is at rest,
The suffering little tree.

75

Dynamic reverie…
Oh, wind!
I wrote this poem
And I will read it,
You, be my only listener,
I want to fly like you
To the end
Of this world,
Accompanied by my beloved
Pine tree.

76

Beam of love…
In a wild bush,
A frog contemplates a mystic tree,
Adagio chants the Heart Sutra:
"Gone, gone, everyone gone
To the other shore."
And praise it,
Then jumps into the air
To hug it.

77

Going into a monologue…
I am talking to you,
But who are you to listen,
Oh! mysterious name
Carved on my trunk,
Against my wish and will,
How you dare
To do that?
It is really not fair!

78

Sweet memory…
On the tree,
A moment
Of a lover’s touch,
And a particular smell
Of love there,
In the air.

79

Dawn of love…
The bright full moon
Moving around a tree
All night long,
What it wants?
This naughty shining one.

80

Self-effacement…
For this Christmas,
On a hermitic tree,
Among the mountains
A great antenna
I have installed,
Through which
The stillness of the universe
Is transmitted,
In the permanent emptiness
And unfolding impermanence.

81

Identity crisis…
A tropical tree,
With dreams wandering
Over a deserted land,
Twirls the silence,
And asks the wind:
"Who am I?"

82

Nostalgic Tree…
I just desire to walk
On my own way
And cross the bridge,
Even over troubled water,
Please do not ask me
In which direction
I have to go,
All roads lead to
The Great Mother Forest,
And sweet cradle, where, as a little seed
I was born.

83

Broken stillness…
Heavens above,
Earth below,
Tree is taciturn,
After scratching away
All the dirt
That accumulated on it,
Sky silent,
But wind is not calm
At all.

84

First light…
Shaking tree,
Fat leaves fall
And lie as they fall,
It is time
To go with the wind,
That is destiny,
That is our life,
Like an old folk tale.

85

Totem pole…
The spirit of
A carved giant effigy
Of the mythical figure,
Rain drips from,
Its green face
Weeps a river of tears,
Ardent to have a new life,
And be a living green tree again
In a tropical rainforest,
What a sturdy resilience!

86

Openness to all sides…
Squirrel lives,
Bird builds nest,
Spider spinning its web,
Tiny ants construct their castles
Close to it,
Man finds shelter and refuge
Under it,
Takes dark carbon
And gives colourless oxygen,
In addition to the tree still
Serene like the wood horse,
Facing the flowers
And the birds.
How it is beautiful!

87

I wish,
Trees in this so chatty world
Could talk,
They must have a lot to say,
They must have tears,
They must have feelings,
And something to say,
Like us.

88

Love everywhere…
On the top of a tree
Two doves in love
Amorously cooing,
I also underneath
Crooning to myself,
And the world.

89

Smell of love…
Visiting a tree,
My young dog
Leads the way,
And with a quick movement
Of its nose
Read an exciting telegram,
On the wet trunk
Left by a female dog,
So in love with him,
Saying:
“Baby puppy, let’s get lost in a crazy love.”

90

Oh! Glorious tree,
Do not bother
By the life's troubles,
You will become useless
Without them.

91

Moment of intense concentration…
Afternoon,
Sitting cross-legged
Like a Buddha,
Me and my shadow,
Under a pine tree
To meditate.

92

Showing compassion…
A wise tree
Whispers
A deep regret
To the young branches,
As the sun goes down,
And the darkness
Reigns again.

93

Autumn is deepening…
Here a plum tree
Standing by itself
Between Heaven and Earth,
Facing infinitude of beings,
All is alone,
Colours of its branches are fading
And leaves are falling down,
But calm and drinks water
From the well of mind,
No visitors it has,
Nor are any expected,
Heart is filled
With melancholy,
And intense anxiety.

94

The hanging Tree…
When the night met
The morning shining sun,
A young peaceful and smart rebel
Against the unjust,
With a rope around the neck
Hanged on an old tree,
Without singing its last
Freedom song,
Branches bow downwards in disgrace,
Weeping bitter tears
For this tragic,
And sad fate.

95

Evening rain…
A violinist sitting
In a treehouse,
Playing the Four Seasons
To the birds,
Branches and leaves,
Broke into rapturous applauses,
Lose the mind,
And go in ecstasy.

96

Victim of love…
My Master
Is always a tree,
I am invincibly attracted to it,
Offering from its dark interior
An essence, which is deep,
And difficult to attain.

97

Pastoral String Quartet…
Tree and branches,
Wind and leaves,
Play Spring Sonata
To the inner ear
Of a deaf composer,
Sheltering from the rain.

98

My legs
Have walked gently
A long distance,
To reach a solitary tree,
Left only with no gain of love,
And my mind returns,
With a million shells.

99

Tree orchestration…
My soul
Is a hidden orchestra,
Roots, trunk, branches and leaves,
Drink a divine sparkling joy,
Blending together to praise,
The earthly happiness,
And splendour of nature's freedom,
I see all of them
With a mind bowing before all,
And moves on,
I sound and clash,
Like my musical instruments
Inside myself.

100

Perfect contentment…
I am a tree,
Standing alone in the field,
Meditate quietly,
When the moon is bright,
My present self is eternally changing,
And my trunk and branches
Heavily wet
With dew.

101

Eternal dilemma…
A thoughtful tree,
Desires to be free
From all kinds of dims
And run away from them,
So, starts to pursuit
Its own shadow,
But discovers that
It can never succeed,
As long as its own existence
Persists,
It got lost with
A smug smile.

102

The face
Of a humble and calm tree
Asked me for a hug,
And kiss,
What a great honour
And sheer joy!

103

Go your own way…
After a secret meeting
Held behind their mother Tree,
Dark and fat leaves
Decide to leave,
To chase the wind,
That is blowing from all sides.

104

Enquiring mind…
A monarch butterfly, perched
On an unknown tree, and asks it,
"How you can see your shadow
Reflected in the water?"
"*When my mind-moon*
Becomes bright,
And my inner eye
Opens wide,"
Said the old and wise Tree.

105

Tree farewell…
The hidden mirror
Under the leaves of my soul,
Raises high
Displays itself,
Blows its horn,
And I see there, my long years
Are broken now
By saw sharp blades,
Of this short and transience nature
Of human life,
And the great way remains,
Too far!

106

In respect
For the sadness
Of the clouds,
We did not celebrate the birthday
Of the cheery tree,
With a young lively bird
Sitting on it,
In the garden.

107

Flowers of emptiness…
Coming and going,
One by one,
Dried branches of a barren fig tree
Breaking and falling silently,
Thinking of nothingness,
From now on.

108

Victim of deformation…
Half tree,
Half dragon,
Feared and loathed by all,
With an anger that
Keeps all far away,
Anxious to be extinct,
And with spirit broken, weeps
Firm and clear whispers:
"All my freedom is lost,
How I can escape from
This whim of fate?"

109

Only God can make a tree…
A gnarled oak tree,
Looks at the sunny God
All day,
And lifts its leafy branches
In solemnity to pray
Before its illumined holy Lord,
Ascends the throne of enlightenment
And loses itself,
In the vast emptiness!

110

Lunatic Tree song…
My spirit
Got strong wings,
And I am going to fly
In the blue sky,
High altitude and more high,
Feeling heavens above,
Heavens below,
I alone am the most honoured one
At this very short moment.

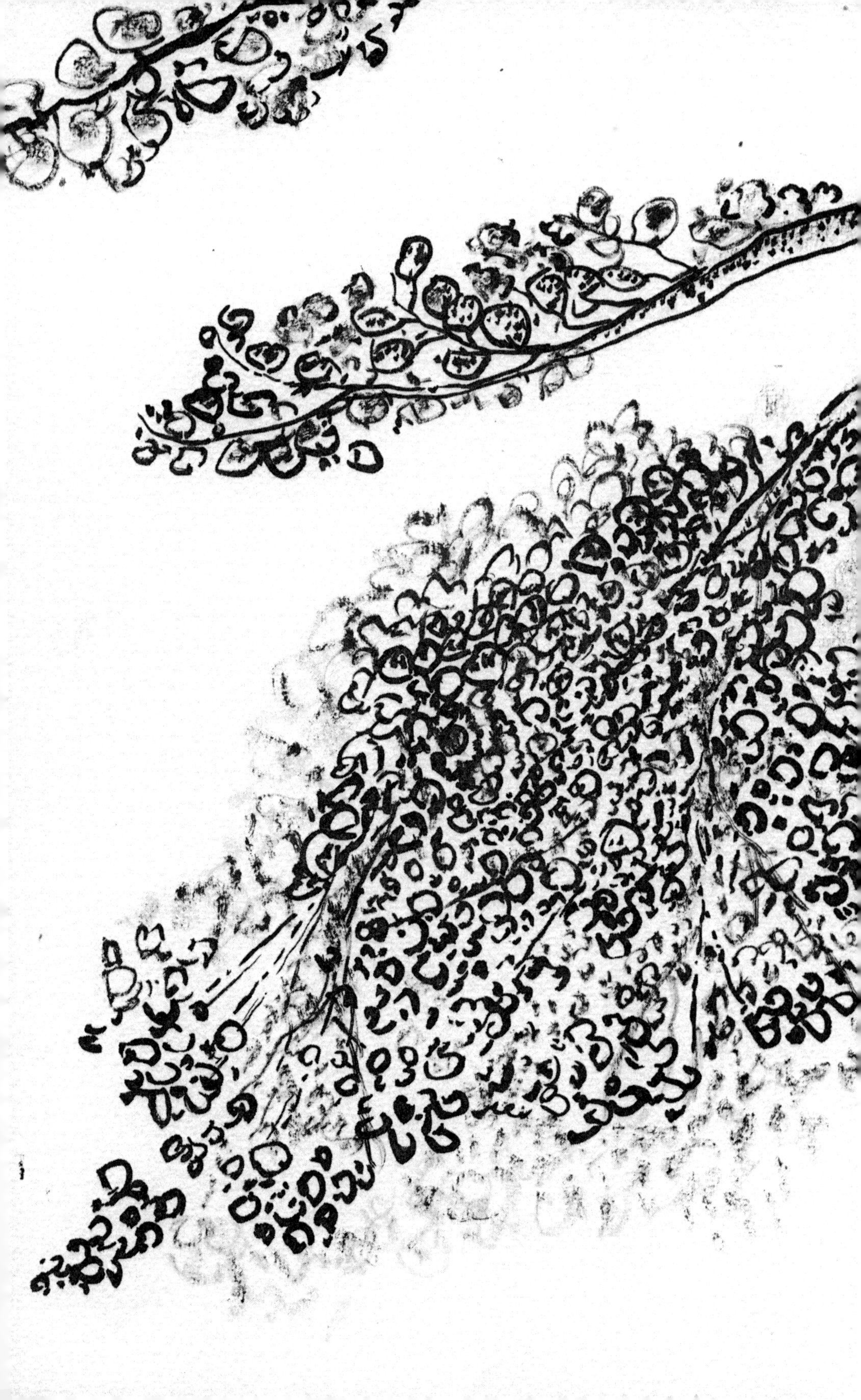

111

It takes two trees to tango…
A wild tree,
With an uncommon colour
Keeping distance enchants it,
From the ordinary turns away
And takes leave,
Enters into the inner side
And loose one's abode,
Virtual partner chooses;
Its soul is a harp,
Beats the strings,
It is tangoing inside,
In the open air.

112

A day of national mourning…
Green flag at half mast,
The silent cry
Of the wind,
A wild tree is dead
With a broken heart,
What a sad day,
For Mother Nature!

113

Grand nature mystic…
In autumn,
A leafless tree
Contemplates in deep silence,
The empty calm footpath
Of the forest,
And goes in ecstasy!

114

Pure spirit…
The roots of a perfect tree
Walk slowly through rocks,
And find no obstacles,
They step on fire
And are not burnt,
Not afraid of all things,
Their nature is unified,
Their spirit is nourished,
And their virtues are harmonised
To consolidate in Oneness,
Nothing can disturb them,
The perfect roots
Soar up above,
The impermanent things!

115

Message in a bottle…
To an unknown tree,
Our love
Is an ancient wild one,
With a forestry heart,
Has no address
And postal code,
And speaks only green language,
That communicates a whiff of
Our Lord Nature's pleasant perfumes!

116

Summer night…
The sound of a darkness and sharp saw,
A young tree falling down,
And singing its last song
Of a floury sweet love;
To the Nature,
To the wind,
To the birds,
To the world.

117

Tree worshipper,
Guardian of yonder field
Far beyond everything,
No thinking,
No reflecting,
No calculating and logic,
In perfect emptiness
I surrounded it
With consecrated ropes,
And I arranged flowers
In form of love,
To protect it
From the evil spirits,
And I pray before it
Chanting a Sutra tree.

118

In this dry orchard,
Silence
Protests against a silent tree,
With a lone bird crying,
Then black silence again!

119

Morning glory…
A gigantic Sequoia Tree,
Finally, ends the last paragraph
About the same shining star
Above it,
Every night.

120

Shrouding tree,
Rustling leaves,
Homeless ghosts
With smiles upon their faces, say,
"Life is a dewdrop,
Fading away
Like a dream in dream."
And one by one, advance
To take the places
Of all earthly things.

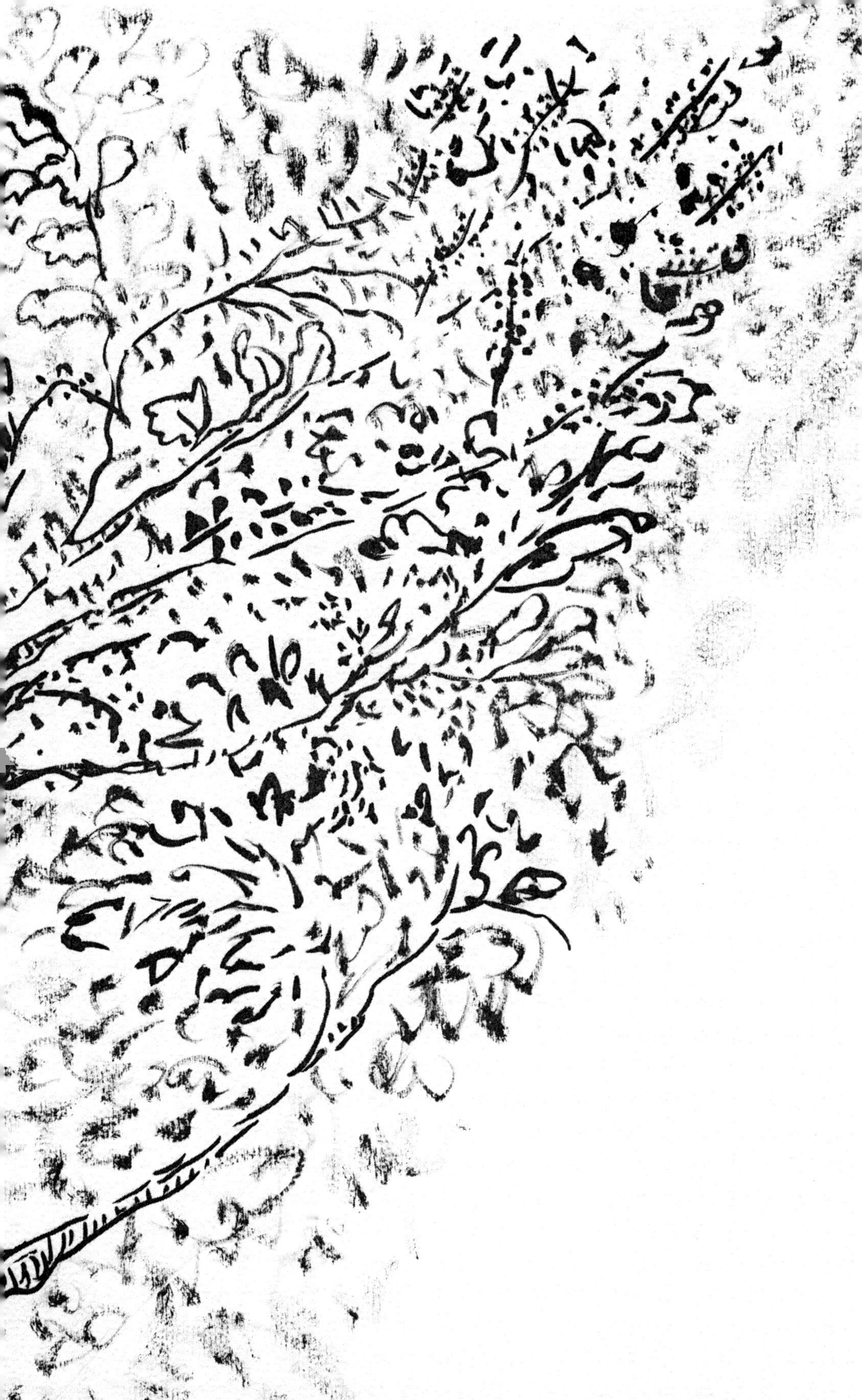

121

Next to a tree,
Lying on the shore
Of my shadow,
I was observing and talking
To the colours
Of my treeness dreams.

122

A real humble tree,
In a wild place
Is one thing
I want to be,
Here and now,
Feeling free and at ease.

123

Mutual withering…
If you really love your tree
Take it with you
When you decide to leave,
How you can breathe sleep and live
Without it?

124

I hold on tight
A wisdom's tree,
And I said:
How do you defend yourself?
"With fantasies and silences,"
Proudly it said.
And rustles softly its leaves
With relief and joy.

125

Free citizen of the world…
Like the spirit
Has no name
And no religion too,
Is there in the afterlife?
A last judgment for a free spirit tree,
I doubt!

126

The green leaves
Of a willow tree
That fall this morning,
Hide the dews
Of last night.
How poetical all that!

127

A caring friend…
Little baby scares
And starts to cry,
The shadow as a guest
Of a loving tree,
Presses its face
On the table.

128

Enchanting young leaves
Of a black tree,
Sing to the dazzling moonlight,
Could their melody
Be sung in other lands,
By other different leaves,
Who knows that?

129

Out of the ordinary…
Birds and wind
Whisper to each other:
"The tree has no words,
But has an inner experience,
Has everything!"

130

Realm of Emptiness…
On a plaque of prehistoric remnant,
A rootless tree
With eyes and ears
And branches asleep,
Grows in confidence
With no conceptualism,
And nowhere to go,
Welcoming change every day,
Not a soul
Ever visits it,
Except, the friendly light
Of the moon,
And a refreshing breeze
Sweeping over all the field,
That makes it
Like a drunken boat,
Adrift from its mooring.

131

Tree for all…
Who is that on my tree?
Angry red squirrel
And naughty woodpecker,
Each claims possession
Of a tree trunk and bark,
Show of a brute force
And fight like a tiger
Over a tree stump,
While the sun smiling
And shining for all,
On Earth.

132

Smile of existence…
Early in the morning,
A flying Tree House
Built on thick trunks,
Surrounded by flourishing branches
In a wild field,
Gives much inspiration
And limitless joy,
The maker is unknown.

133

Somewhere I know…
I wander alone as clouds,
That float on high
Over trees in an empty field,
I came across a fallen tree
Gazing and gazing,
I felt it's sad flowering branches
Look at me, and say:
"You are falling also into loneliness again."
I did meet
My first love,
In that little place
A long time ago.

134

Every day is a new good day…
Well, well,
I think always,
Yesterday, today, and tomorrow
Are the same for a tree
With growing branches and leaves,
Like Arabic letters
Hanging in the air,
But today, I realised that,
It has within,
So flourishing and vivid spirit also!

135

Autumn exchanged glances…
Ruins of ancestral Triumphal Royal Arch
Rusty unknown statue,
Flowered tree
Give a smile,
Look towards them,
And vice versa.

136

Tree tender and touching…
Oh! Little woodlice
Insects that sing
In the field,
My thick trunk,
Would really be
A place of refuge
For you here,
So, welcome my dear friends.

137

Wishful thinking…
Oh! My beloved tree,
Was I perhaps
Your relative in a former life,
Please, when I die
Be the guardian of my ashes,
Till we will meet again,
In another better world.

138

Green Polytheism…
Trees send out
Their growing branches
In all directions,
To enquire the falling
Of a friendly shining star,
Last night.

139

Softly soaring…
Two wise redwoods,
Messengers of illumination
That experience the strongest winds,
Approach the far,
And give shade and hospitality
To the stranger,
Meet in a barren landscape,
They smile broadly and ask:
"Having no blossoms and fruit,
Is it a sign of life,
Without a shining love's light?"
Then they climb up,
With one love and heart
Onto the dream space,
To reach the sky, and kiss
The holy sun's face.

140

Together forever…
Oh, pretty little tree,
When the world is reduced
To a pile of ruins,
And you are swept away
By the high seas,
I will find you,
And heart to heart
By the open sea,
We will wander aimlessly,
Around the world,
Till the end.

141

Tree birthday party…
Not being able to dance,
It shakes
It's branches, singing:
"Happy birthday to me."

142

Metamorphosis…
A tree,
Absent of selfhood
Is growing near my window,
It's large poor leaves
Are torn by a fierce storm,
Becoming like a beggar's robe,
All in tatters,
In them, I see
Myself
In this world.

143

Intimate loveliness…
Everyone else gone to sleep,
But the moon remains
All night,
With the lovely olive tree,
There is nothing between them,
Sharing little moments,
Little things,
Which are not little at all!

144

The magic flute…
I plant
A tropical bamboo,
So, the wind can make
A divine harmonious music,
And the tree can hear,
And enjoy!

145

Global environmental pollution…
A rebelled young tree
Collects all its own growing branches,
Fat green leaves and perfumed flowers,
And departs to find a dreamland
With no sinful souls.
So-called The Land of Purity,
Where everything is clear and right,
And every moment is
A new rebirth,
And a new experience.

146

Tree funeral…
What a silent agony,
Heart shaded with regret,
For the sacrifices
Of a dead dried tree.
In the annual posterity
Who shall represent its sufferings?
And what it has endured.
Who rapports how much
The other trees venerated it?
Who shall bear a kindle,
Raises a tree flag,
And shout: "*Viva!*"
Who, if someone will ask,
What happened to the tree?
Will say:
"It has gone to the next world,
On some treeness business."

147

Stormy night…
People are asleep,
And all is as usual,
A tree all night
Slowly dancing and sparkling,
With a gusty wind.

148

Avoiding to be hurt…
Behind a friendly and silent tree,
I find a secure refuge
To hide myself,
When an impromptu force,
Throws up all sorts of troubles
On my face
From everywhere.

149

Solitude…
Forever, this tree
All along the day,
Not saying a word,
Standing on the hill,
Casting its shadow
With a stillness that abides,
In the present.

150

Bridging the gap between lovers…
A pretty Cherry blossom tree,
Living in wetter soils
Falls in love with another tree,
In the opposite bank
Of a flowing river,
How pathetic is that!

151

Tree compassion…
A young growing flower shoot
Begins to break through,
Tree orders its outstretching branches,
To protect it
From the gusty wind,
That is blowing hard!

152

Aria…
I have a lovely tree
In my soul,
Whispers poems to the rain,
And with the bright sunrise,
Sweet sounds of birds of passage
On the top of it
Sing from the chest,
Of my childhood
I have a tree in my memory,
Where none can touch
And reach it,
I have the beauty of Earth.

153

Be like a tree…
Every day with a new concern,
Never stops with one experience,
Changes its leaves
Like different opinions,
But it keeps intact,
The roots.

154

Nature Postal Service…
Today,
No letter,
No message
From the lover,
A tree complains
To the Green Lord against
The naughty wind,
What a treeness bothersome and worry!

155

As if in a nightmare…
A pretty tree won't let me
Become a flower,
What a thorny one,
I am really in this world!

156

When I have decided to not marry,
How I envy
Two trees in love,
With branches strongly intricated,
And leaves touch and kiss each other.
The autumn of my life!

157

Stony time…
A summer day,
Two solid tall columns of cement
Looking enviously
At the same flourishing tree,
What a hard and stony destiny,
Of a postmodern time!

158

Fantasy tree…
From the beautiful land
Of my beloved tree,
I have brought an amulet,
Perfumed by the fragrance
Of its leaves net,
And unseen sensor of lust.
To protect my unleashed
Down soul fate,
Knocking every day,
On my broken old door.

159

Christmas mirage…
To an ardent devout,
Wandering aimlessly
In a remote desert,
God appears like
An evergreen Christmas tree,
Takes his hand
For dancing to Handel's
'Water music.'

160

A peaceful settlement research…

Tree:

My soul is like
A mirror bright,
But is not yet pacified.

Wind:

Bring your soul,
I will clean it and
Let not dust collect upon it,
And I will have it pacified,
Once for all!

161

Genocide of trees…,
The tropical forest
Turns to a desert
The world becomes nothing,
Struggling poor soul
In a wild veld,
Oxygen in the air
Little left,
And the gift of Mother Nature
Has its own tears.
Deforestation!

162

All you need is a tree…
A lone small tree,
Growing everyday
Taller and taller,
Bigger and wider,
Standing surrounded by cut trees,
Whispers of Wisdom
Of unknown source,
Shaded with regret in the air:
'Yet each one kills the thing he loves,
And let this be heard.'

163

Kiss to all the trees…
Under the blessed Tree's shade,
With joy of union,
And gentle touch
Of green branches,
Kissing and embarrassing the tree,
Make the whole kin
And taste deep inside
Brotherhood in greenness,
In mind,
In heart,
And in spirit too!

164

Spring…
New season's fashion,
Colour of the tree
Has a change of clothes
And face,
It is an Ode to beauty!

165

Tree of Liberty…
I live among the others,
But when I battle against
The army of hatred,
And the mob of unloving,
I yearn to the lonely tree,
Living in the wilderness area,
In a world of dreams,
And fantasia!

166

Royal solitude…
An unknown tree
Stands next to
A lone unfrequented path,
Evergreen,
Casts its shadow,
And its deep breaths
For many years abides there,
No one knew it,
And gives it a title and name.

167

Utter extinction…
A remarkable friendly tree,
Whispered to me
About its love for a smart bird,
Built a warm nest
In its ample bosom,
Branches bent all over him
To prostrate with joy,
But has left his nest
To join the light,
And obtain deliverance
From all worldly attachments,
And sufferings.

168

Frankincense…
In the temple of the moon,
Tears of the tree
Deep wounds and
Cruel fate has inflected it.
Still bleeding,
For rare and precious gift
Poured out,
To serenade mind and heart,
Gospel of Sweet Wind,
Dove of inspiration for thoughts,
And fragrance of faith,
Calling to forget
And forgive always.

169

Dreamy experience…
This very earth
Is the land of purity and sweet melodies.
I do not hear with ears,
I hear with heart,
And I speak with unsound mind
In an unsound body.
I do not change all that and disappear.
I am not God,
I am not demon,
A little sun air and water,
And all my branches are blooming.
My body and soul,
Are married by Mother Nature.
In the creation,
And all that I behold,
Is full of blessings.
I knelt down,
And I become the gardener of
This reverend awakened Guru Tree.

170

Gracious Majesty…
For a companion,
On my last journey of life
I would like to have a tree.
With an alluring smile,
Walking beside me
And my green coffin,
Till the last breath of life.
In this transient world!

171

With respect…
In a tropical forest,
I drink a toast
Of a silent glass,
With myself alone
In company of my heart.
To praise the trees,
The perch of common birds,
And the Holy Sea of
Nature's Golden Throne.
Without them my whole world
Turns misty.

172

Treeless place…
Throughout this arid land,
There is no tree
For migrating birds to perch,
And have a warm nest.
All things are void,
Myself and the rest.
Both my ears are deaf,
And my tongue is died.
Only spring breeze,
And an inseparable nothingness,
Attached to me,
That can’t get away.
Even while I am relaxed,
And writing these verses.

173

Broken true tall tree,
Without name and title.
In pure quietude,
With empty wind song in it.
Falls gently over the field
Of sleepless grass,
In the forest of light
And universal unity.

174

In the blue void,
An ancient and lonely tree
That supports the sky
Stands on the wet grass.
With inner freedom,
Watching its years.
Flow under an old bridge,
Enveloped in grey mist,
With spacious mind.

175

Enlightened tree…
The water inside me,
Listening to the sounds
Of wisdom
That comes from an unknown source,
And abyss of loneliness.

176

Windy field,
An ancient tree,
Like a horse
Rearing up,
And lulling a sleepless
Verge of dawn.

177

Who knows its tree knows itself…
This is my beloved family tree.
My fate is intimate with it.
Which kind of bird
Am I?
Lost identity,
And mind,
Homeless forever.
With a sense of desolation,
Accompanied by wild dreams.

178

Time to rest and love…
Next to an ignored tree.
The unashamed touches
And warm stolen kisses
Of two naughty lovers
Performed there.
In the treetop,
Funny two birds of passage.
It was so curious all that,
For them.

179

Somewhere,
There is a tropical forest.
Where a tree
Covered with grey mist,
As I approach it,
A white butterfly
Wraps me in light,
And guides me
All the way!

180

Unwilling solitude…,
Voiceless naked tree
Planted in the centre town.
Standing lonely,
With elegant shape.
All its branches are outlined,
Trembling in the fierce breath
Of the infinite.
Yearning for another,
To meet and talk,
In this middle summer day.

181

Wisdom tree…
Tree of the Universe,
Its boughs stretched up into heaven,
They spread out into the branches.
Its roots reach down into the dark regions
Beneath the earth.
Pure water spirit rises
Through the fountain of its trunk
And evaporate from its crown,
In a mystical watery transcendental journey.
And come back as a rain,
Fragrant and sun loving.
A teaching tree of enlightenment
And wise understanding,
Bright and always clean,
No dust and dirt,
Collected upon it.
It is the tree of time and life,
It is a mystic true tree,
Without label, title and rank.

182

Impermanence…
Giant redwood
Grows so high,
As to reach the sky,
Leaves falling down,
Return to the roots,
And disappear.
Then generously incarnate again.
Hare Tree! Hare Rama!

183

Tree immigration…
A little floating seed
Equipped with tiny invisible wings.
Powerful storm
Carries it for miles,
And lands
Outside the forest,
To be stranger in a foreign land.
Grows up alone as far away,
From its mother old tree.
It is a season of rebirth,
And flourishing hope,
Elsewhere.

184

Light food…
A small tree
In the dim light,
In a race
For a place,
In the sun,
It is time to feed.

185

It is a new day…
A hermit rounded tree,
Little wants to do
With others.
Isolated by its silence,
Every day in the forest,
Is a discovery and a learning day,
For it.

186

To know a tree is to become a tree…
A light breeze passes by,
Stirring the leaves
And ceaselessly knocking
On an old tree trunk,
Hoping to enter right into the inside.
Birds find that so funny,
And laugh quietly at me.
I am ignorant with knowing;
Loveless with loving,
Dark with light.
And my mind like
A gourd on water
Floating all time in and out.
Of all kinds of thoughts
Waiting to open for me
The door of its mystery.
To allow me to depict its spirit,
And listen to its internal voice
From the inside.

187

Hopefulness…
Lonely tree,
In an arid place
Standing still
And being there all time.
Without leaves and cortex,
Without friends and neighbours,
Thirsty and wanting to drink,
Patient and happy,
Holding a nest
With a lonely heart,
Sings for the new life.

188

Treeness epiphany…
While my eyes
Are opened by the sound
Of the church bell.
I asked a Guru pine tree,
Holy in spirit and protected
By its outstretched branches,
To lend me its wisdom.
It whispered something in my ear:
"*Renew yourself every day,*
And if you have nothing to create,
Perhaps create yourself."
That is all I got from it.

189

Apostle of poverty and solitude…
In the stillness of a forest,
There stands
A solitary old young tree.
Fresh and green all year round,
With strong roots,
Firmly set in the ground,
Trunk is hollow inside,
Sighing softly to the flowers,
Ardently wants a lover.
While its young branches,
Reach for the sky,
And the timeless eternity.
Pitiful indeed this special tree!

190

It is a new dawn…
Tree of the morning
Looking for a warm light
To wear.
And new truth
To enter its mind.
In this new dawn
Of a sunny day.

191

It is too cold.
My hands start to shake
Like leaves.
I see you through the window,
I wish we could touch,
And hug each other,
To keep warm.
Oh! Gnarled old olive tree.

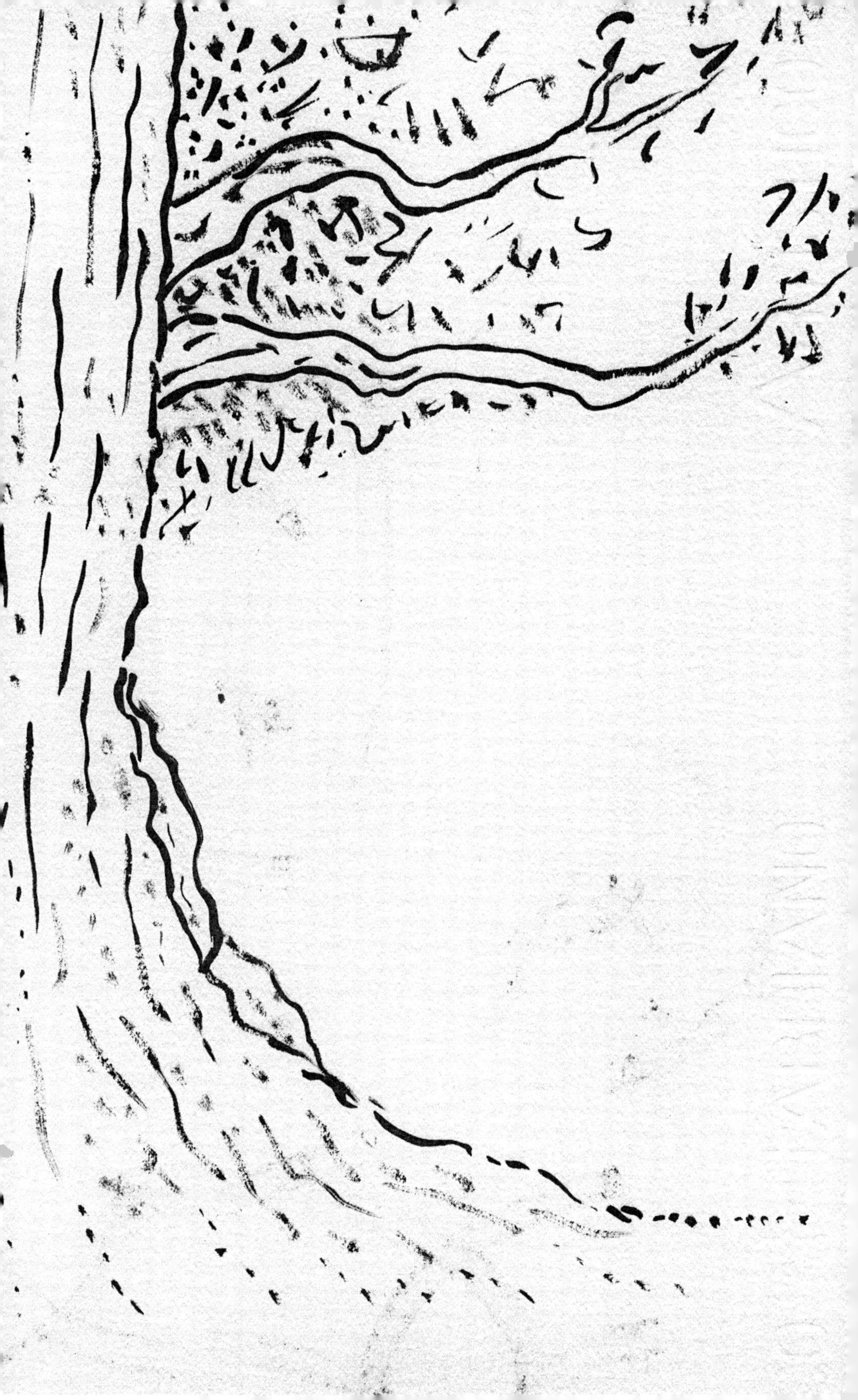

192

Climb up into the tree of belief…
Roots above,
And top below,
Branches and buds grow downwards.
Rooted in godhead,
It turns inwards,
In its own mind.
To have a glimpse into
Its own self-nature.
And to understand
The inner words and wisdom
Of the eternal spirit,
Hidden in the forest
Of the soul,
It is a real transcendental Tree.

193

Years of solitude…
A single crooked tree
With twisted branches,
Planted in a deserted street.
Trembling in each breath,
Fragrant leaves yearning
For another tree,
To love!

194

The light is within thee…
An old Guru
Seating in the shade of a tree,
Teaches his pupils patiently.
How to get out of suffering,
And arises the wisdom,
Asleep within.
So, teach on Master
And let minds adopt,
The misty thoughts.

195

Sharing compassion…
Leaves of two old wise trees
Are relinquished without regret,
Spontaneously fall
Undisturbed on a narrow path,
In the deep green void,
That leads to a new harmony,
Between the opposites.
To heal the destructive force
Of hatred lust and illusion,
Utterly beyond thought!

196

Suchness…
All trees
Are from the same essence,
Like ice and water.
They tear the veils of illusion,
And perceive their original face and
Hearing the voice of silence,
With the cosmic eyes.
Each one is a mirror of life,
A book of holy goodness,
And sacred land of purity.
Trees never get tired
Of each other.
A real consecrated treelogy!

197

Trees alphabet…
Planted words,
Flourishing leaves,
Forking branches,
Bursting buds,
From the substance of
The inner bark of the tree
Are alphabet and words.
Create a meaning
And potential stories,
To be deciphered in the woods.
Tree is an effective and eloquent speaker.
And I showered it with praise,
And pure love.

198

Nesting season…
Today, the trees are sad,
And bending out of shape.
Without bird chatter,
And capricious cacophony,
Then suddenly disappear
In a thick fog.
And sink into the silent valley
Of absolute emptiness.

199

Naked union…
God sleeps in a tree
Like twins blended in one.
And to the tree's inner ear
Speaks of compassion love and wisdom.
Tree's soul hears and remembers,
While it is bathing
In the sunlight of the spirit,
Unseen by anyone.
Save the eye of the soul,
Free from the web of delusion,
And despair.

200

Heatwave and drought,
A tree gazes over the field
With heart watches and receives,
Seeks and finds nothing.
Sees everywhere the same things,
Void of a real existence.

201

Stressful situation…
Drops off its flowers,
And changes its colour
Waiting for a new life
Right and fair,
To come in that open air.
A young lemon tree!

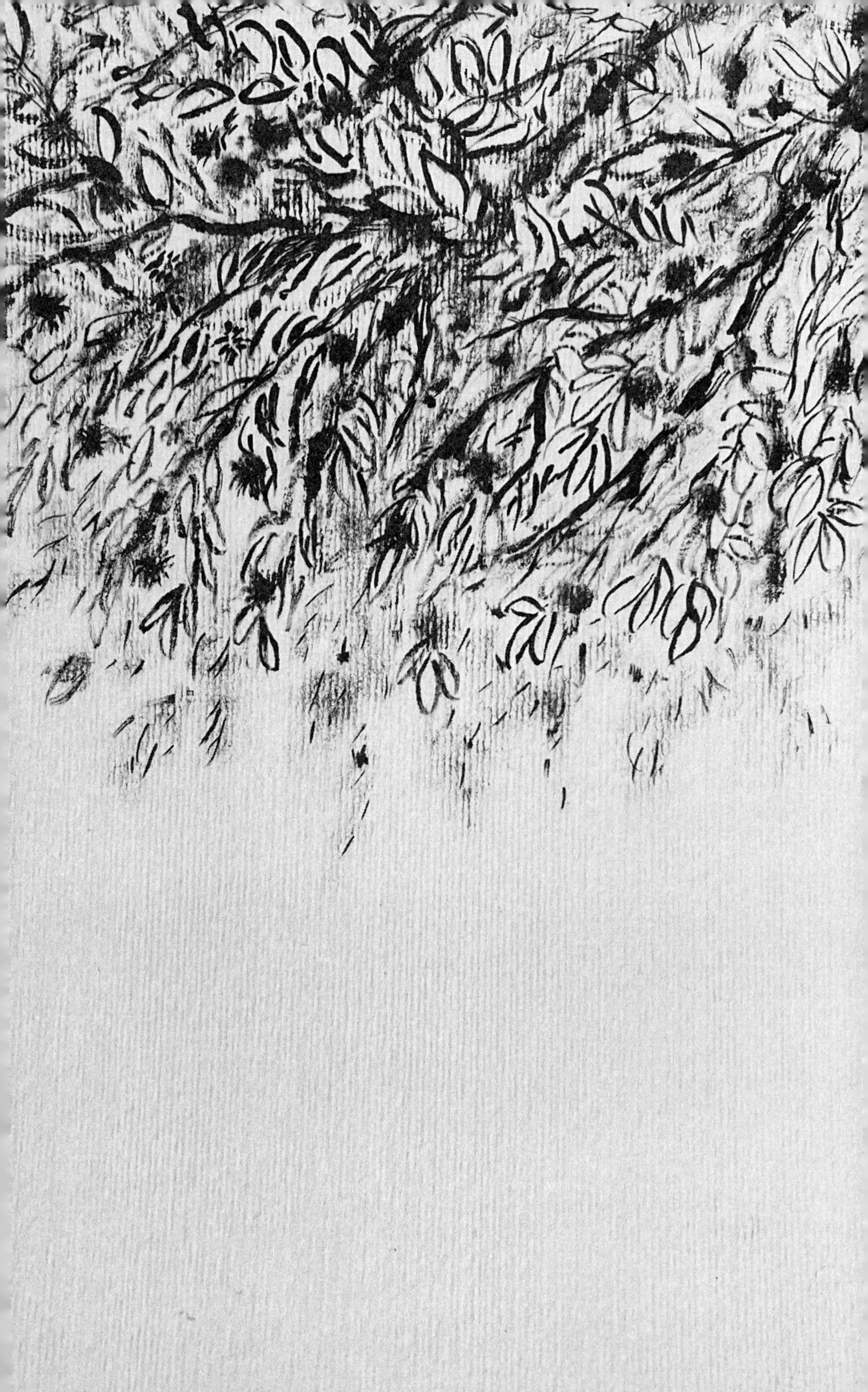

202

A withered tiny tree
Of no worth and value,
Offers its heart's flowers,
To anyone who passes,
Every day and hour.
They are colourful flowers
Of the soul.

203

The birth of music in the tree…
In order to compose
And gives an authentic spirit to its work,
A creative deaf musician,
With a great imaginative spirit of enquiring
Who loves tree more than man,
Enters right into a beautiful tree.
To know:
All its secrets,
All its joy,
All its sufferings,
All its inner sounds and music.
He becomes a tree,
It becomes a musician,
Both are now a mirror to each other.
Is it a musician's dream to be a tree<
Or a tree's dreams to be a musician?
How marvellous all that!

204

Christmas Tree…
Cold wind blows,
Seems to have no end,
Darkness descends,
Tropical depression goes on,
A lonely white Christmas tree
With silver and red leaves
Proudly erected there.

All-loving supreme pagan God,
Dressed all in green,
Lying too deep inside it
Standing in the middle of a forest,
As an original purity which
Abides in a silent stillness.
In the present,
To celebrate a new year.

Nothing of thinking and perceiving,
But only strong feelings.
Roots, trunk and branches,
And all in all,
One in nature,

Tuned together to the vast
Oneness.
Not separated from the ground
Where it comes and belongs.
Plunged into an unbroken stillness
With a silence roars like thunder,
To celebrate a new vibrating life,
With a light shining in itself,
Lit up by a sweet
Guardian angel's smile.

Parakeet duet
With bright feathers,
Nested on the top of it
Shake their long tails,
And gracefully sing:
"All we want for Christmas is a long life,
To our beloved and generous
True Tree."

What a night, divine tree
Of no rank and title
Standing there always,
Day and night.
It cannot do otherwise,
But feeling over the moon,
'Secret' is its name.

205

Woods wild vocabulary…
Trees are words planted
To create meaning,
And seed stories,
In the beauty of greenness
Of the existence book.

206

Liberating reverie…
Upright pine tree,
Child of earth and water,
A static being
Intoxicated with uprightness,
And landscapes of the soul.
Model of heroic verticality
And aerial purity.
In an inner peace
Never ever lie down.
Its leaves rustling
In quiet and silence,
Are like innumerable wings.
Carries terrestrial life
To the nursing blue sky.
Looking for light and sun
Like a dreamer poet,
Who praises the sacred height,
Searching for enlightenment,
And experience of transcendence of being,
In an aerial imagination.

207

Nocturnal dream…
An ardent meditating being,
Leaning with his whole body
And thought
Against a young nut tree,
With its inner sun honey
Shoulder to shoulder,
Back to back,
Breast to trunk,
Soul to soul,
Both entering in an ecstasy
Of ascension,
Within a vastness that reconciles,
The contraries.

208

Oak tree…
It ties itself in knots
To support its own weight.
It is hard, so it can lift
It's airy crown.
Its high, winged foliage
To give a towering image
Of legitimate pride,
With knotty and twisted trunk
To support its own weight.
Like a monk who has twisted his nature
In fervent and wilful prayer.
It is a toughness achieved only
By turning in upon itself.
Happy who looks full,
Of beauty and strength.

209

Space of infinity…
If you want to be a tree,
Create an inner space
For it inside you,
With love and care.

210

Springtime…
Today, I washed my window,
Now I see the tree in my garden.
So green and looks like a dream castle,
It is a cradle for birds,
Then natural light enters
In the house,
And sit across the room,
Bright in its stillness.

211

Arbour Day…
My hands plant a tree
In a wild unknown land.
It will grow in its full glory,
And be friend with the moon.
Will gives soft nutrient fruits,
Even when not admired.
Birds will come sure
To build nests on it,
And dream of new happy chicks,
With minds free of ties
Of all idle thoughts,
And sensations of pain
Just flying and singing,
In the open air.
And moving all around,
From place to place
To create the world,
That they themselves are.
What a day of pure joy!

212

Experiencing the awareness…
I see the beauty
Of an old olive tree,
I see a soft inner light,
I see that each thing in it
Contains within itself,
All things,
And I see branches growing out
From the main stem,
With flourishing fat leaves,
Driving away the evil spirits,
Symbols of peace,
As well as sharing unity
And the split between Me.
And not Me
Is healed,
Is suspended,
Is disappeared.
How boundless and wise
This divine tree.
Of the world!

213

Fleeting vision of a Tree…
Aerial life
A wild emigrated seed
Planted by the wind,
Next to a river,
Became a flourishing tall tree.
Caring greenness to the sky,
With flowers spreading all around,
And homeless birds nesting
In the top.

Tinge of sadness
Grows alone and in a full roundness
With solitude as only friend,
And a wounded young soul,
Has no other love than its own shadow
Reflected in a clear and deep water,
That calls for a seeing in-depth
And going beyond too.

In the obscure night,
Seeds of doubt in the mind,
Thoughts refuse to settle,
While the shy full moon above
Watching with a smiling face.
Then decided to abandon and forget,
All life's unpleasant worries,
And go deep inside it,

Looking for light and
Hope to find inner peace.
But finds nothingness,
Open and vast,
Empty and lucid.

Back to nature
Stands firmly gazing around
In all directions,
Then sings softly a song
To be awakened in life,
With sounds of rustling leaves
On a breezy night.
What a coming back!

214

Life of quietness and inner purity…
I stand,
Face to face
With a cypress tree
In a mountain field.
Just a glimpse of me
And we are in love?
We are undivided,
I am in it,
I am it and it is I,
And at the same time,
I am I am and it is it.
I fixed it with an unwavering stare,
I touched it intimately with my hand,
With a mind watches,
And receives.

215

A willing tool…
Trees pushes itself out
On the Earth
Like hair on the skin,
From its root
To define the space and itself,
Tree upward groping
For the bright light,
Its twisting,
Its struggling,
Its reaching against all resistances
Towards the sun,
branches wrest themselves away
From the parental trunk,
To find its own way,
Fight against the elements
And fly high,
To explore the mysteries
Of the sky.

216

Tree's inquietude…
Myriad of leaves
To be blown away
A little earlier
A little later.

Some other leaves had already fallen,
Many remained stunted,
Some were still freshly green,
Slender twigs sweep like a girl's hair
In the gentle breeze,
But soon the wind sweep
Would all away.

Then after the tortures of frost,
There would follow
A new explosion of pink blossoms,
Then leaves again!
And next autumn the branches
Would once more bend down,
Under burdens of fruits.
How many times tree
Sees spring departs,

Sees winter comes again,
See restlessness going ahead?

The tree is like a mankind
Full of worries and thoughts,
And makes us to see into it
As a real being,
Rooted deep in the Earth.

217

Inner activity…
Tree pushes itself out
Of the earth,
Like hair on the skin
From its roots,
To define the space
And itself too
It picks up
And leaves out forms and details,
Tree upward groping
For the bright pure light,
Its twisting
Its struggling
Its reaching against all obstacles,
And high and low resistances,
Towards the sun.
Free young branches,
Wrest themselves away
From the parental trunk,
To find their own way,
Fight against the elements
And fly high,
To explore the blue sky.
What a willing tool!

218

United by Mother Nature…
We are not thus isolated
Living in ghettos separated from the rest,
Or creatures dancing through a world,
Blunted by lies and wide repetitions,
And divided by ghostly mental walls.

We are in fact, all naturally interrelated
All the same,
Like the tree and the man
All are the same dust
Of the planet Earth,
Both spring from the ground,
Both will have the same final outcome,
All return to dust
From where they came.

So, let us go beyond the exterior chaos
And strip the veil of identity
From the world,
Which obscures from us,
The wonder and beauty
Of the sleeping connection.

Let us getting to the heart of inherent
And intuitive knowledge,
Let us purge our inward sight
And create a new world,

Where evil is out of place
Goodness is to be worshipped and installed,
And all that we behold
Is full of blessings and joy.
We will find,
That we are all deeply connected
In the ample bosom of Mother Nature,
Warmly open for all,
And its gift of a harmonious spirit
To alleviate divisions and sufferings.

And when connection is happened,
Everything becomes luminously clear,
Funny and very fair.
Togetherness is our destiny and friend!

219

Homeliness feeling…
I imagined myself to be a tree,
Talking to my pretty neighbour tree,
I asked it: *"Who we are?"*
If really you want to know that,
We are originally one emptiness,
Abiding in an unsophisticated simplicity.
Neither good nor bad,
Neither true nor untrue,
We are like rain hail and snow,
Ice too, are set apart
But when they fall
The same water of the valley stream,
That nourishes you and me
By sweet and freshwater
Drawn up through our roots.

220

Life of inner quietness and purity…
I stand
Face to face
With a cypress tree,
In a mountain field
Just a glimpse of me,
And we are in love?
We are now undivided,
I am in it,
I am it and it I,
And at the same time
I am I and it is it,
What is, is not,
What is not, is,
As the two sides of one sheet of paper
That is one and yet is two,
It like light
Containing all colours in it
But itself colourless,
I fixed it with an unwavering stare,
I touch it intimately with my hand,
With a mind that watches and receives
Its great divine grace!

221

A family reunion…
For a brief moment,
Two falling and lost leaves
Merging from the fog,
The wind brought them together
Close to their mother tree.

222

Dreamland treelogy…
I saw trees
Coming towards me,
Jumping, as in a dance,
Trunks without stopping
Move from form to form,
Move out of the field of vision
But not vanishing,
All are like the same tree,
All were myself
And in all trees is shown,
The treeness veiled,
And as if in a riddle!

223

Tree nobility…
Over the Earth,
Over the roots
And flourishing branches
Over myself
And the rest,
Over the leaves
I bend like a rainbow
Of pure compassion and love,
To embrace all.

224

When tree goes out of existence…
A fire lighting in the sky,
Tree masterpiece of Nature
Is bursting in flames,
Burning strong, very bright
Sounds of cracklings are heard,
Family of green fat leaves
Weep widely over this sealed fate
And tragedy strikes.
In a world of illusions,
Condemned by a compulsory return
To an empty nothingness,
Where everything started.
The glowing black ashes
Drift away in a vast space
By the blowing wind,
Distant cry and rage
Of Mother Nature,
In the air.

225

Angel looking for legs…
In a spotless dreamy orchard,
A young tree asked a wise tree:
“What shall we do when thoughts
Move always and never stop
Raising and disappearing?”
“Be cold ashes,
And a withered tree.”
“What is the eternal and
fundamental principle of things?”
“Movement,” it replied
“What is this movement?”
“When you see things move.”
The tree was lost in thought and said:
“We do not move.”
“So, we are still in the dust
Of this world
It is just like this.”

226

Impermanence...
Beauty is often fleeting and fade away,
An oak tree
With a sweet fragrance
Lives a thousand years,
Lilly flowers, brightly coloured
Last just one day,
But time sooner or later comes,
And in one of those unusual, damned days
Both fulfil their destiny and depart forever,
And the curtain of the tragic-comic transient life
Goes silently down
And die at the end,
Becoming like silent bones
No longer have selves,
Dropped to their death
And thrown like stones,
What a reward to be reaped,
After all numerous good things
That have been done!

227

Unselfishness…
A true tree
Without label and rank,
Without title and status,
Without distortion,
Suffused with light
And a genuine humility,
Planted next a lake
To hold together the earth,
The shore and fresh air.

228

Elevation…
I changed
My new furnished flat
For a pretty tree house
Built on a solid oak tree,
On the side of a hill
Overlooking the river
I called it, 'Waiting the Moon!'

On high of it
I installed a great antenna,
Through which
The stillness of the vast silent universe
Andante molto espressivo is transmitted,
Accompanied by the sweet sounds of
'Clair de moon' by Debussy,
And it travel heavenly notes
That adapt themselves to the lyrical effusions
Of the soul,
And fantasy of the soul!

229

A single Palm Tree
No one knows who first planted it,
A creature with soul,
It talks but impossible to understand
Its own words,
Here to stay
Night and day,
Firm and erect
Its roots are sunk
In the terrace of white sand,
It is free from dust and mud
Delighted of being alone,
Now that I have come to visit it,
It has loosened the shackles,
That binds my heavy heart.

230

Song of a pagan Tree…
I want to be planted
On a pretty swing
As a sweet mobile homeland,
And not in a barren field
Moving from side to side,
Either in and out
Always in between,
By not being a part of anything
And nothing must chain me,
Here, there and everywhere.

I want to walk on this earth
With extra-long and strong legs,
And enjoy the air that I breathe
With my branches as compass,
And happy sincere smiles on my face,
I want to be like migratory birds
That softly sing to the passing clouds,
Flying from place to place
And never ever fear,
Cold and roaring fire
In any space.
I want to drown myself
In the silence of absence,
Wherever roses grow
In the garden of love,
And write lyrical poems
Of inner greenness at best,

And never being tired of myself.

I want to be weightless,
Forever out of place
And remain where I am,
In a lasting peace
Feeling good and free,
Praying and worshipping the Mighty Sun
Without words and sacred verses,
Belonging to the past and today.
What a remarkable Tree!

231

Trees romantic love in the Boulevard…
In a wide street
With trees lined in either side,
Two trees sway along the breeze
Like pretty little leaves,
Secretly talk
And intimately whisper
Through the day,
It is a birth of treeness love!

Invitation to dance
Both very much like to dance this night,
By the light of a bright full moon
While the rest of the trees are deeply sleep,
Accompanied by a blowing wind
That shall neither caught nor caged,
Moving slowly from side to side
And increasing the grace,
Never touch each other
Here and there.

Fungi at the bottom of Mother Earth
Link them through the roots
And connect in togetherness,
Their mutual feeling,
And deep affection
All the way.

Fresh fruits glittering in the sunlight,
And still clinging to the branches
Shine and shake with small flashes of light
And a particular emotion,
Fearless of wind or rain
Fat green leaves
Flap like wings of birds,
Like flags in the air
To salute and celebrate,
This new love and pure joy
With rustling sweet sounds,
Too ardent for a hug
And a warm treeness kiss,
Then sing a sweet love song
That trembles with desire, love and hope,
The winds become words,
And walk between tree and tree.

232

A pretty violin,
Newly born from a mute tree
With hidden sweetness,
That grows in tonal quantity,
And sing softly,
To ease a rustic heart!

233

Song without words…
Leaves of an Oka tree
Rustle and dance,
Feel so good and free
In the breeze,
Like a love song that they create,
Like a pastoral green symphony,
On the nature stage.

234

Tree lamenting on a remote mountain…
In this world of dreams and possibilities
Many things exist,
Many transient things disappear
Here and there.
Who am I?
I hear no answer yet,
Only birds are singing
And a wind is soughing,
My life goes on.
I am standing here alone,
Loneliness pierces me all the while,
My mind goes on wandering,
And I know that all this
Will end in an absolute nothingness,
I live as long as I am allowed to,
How long should I remain lamenting
And how I can contain myself?

235

Wilderness…
A wild tree,
Wild as the wind,
As the stars and the birds,
And the shining moon,
And wild also within,
Said to me:
"We have more in commune
More than setting us apart,
Words won't wait
Write, write, write,
About us in serene,
And about our deep connection."

236

Intimate relationship…
Upon the dark night
Dawn comes to smile,
Leaves are flying up and down
Here I feel free as the air,
I sit with eyes closed
Wearing only one robe,
Whispering and speaking
And singing loudly with a pine tree,
Standing alone on the hill
I cut off my ties with the world,
Thus, its troubles will fade away,
I see only the moon
Hanging far above
Now and then,
I will do this again and again,
As long as life stay with me,
With or without rain.

237

Being more than a Tree…
Oh, pleasant solitude,
You do you,
Sanctuary refuge and place of retreat,
What the sages have seen and found in you?
Firmly rooted in one spot
Standing and still,
Trunk bowing down
As an act of genuine humility,
With branches out in life
Unrestrained and fury,
Moving dancing with the wind
Fat green leaves,
All are in movement,
Under a spell of pure joy!

238

Archetypal tree…
In the heart of a little seed,
Deeply buried and sweetly asleep,
A little pretty tree
Wake up said the sun to it,
The rain is dropping
And creep to the light to see,
What a wonderful outside
The new world!

239

Plant a tree…
The tree is not just individual
That has one of its own,
It is also a page
And has an interesting story to tell,
Endued with true wisdom
And unmindful of good and bad,
In this world.

240

Tree is roofless
Yet the rain does not wet it,
Nor the wind strike it,
It is simply calm and firm
In its own native place,
Hopping under the umbrella of unity
Of nature and humanity,
All can live in prosperity and peace.

241

In a world of grief and pain
Tree flourishing even there,
He who plants a tree,
He plants hope and love.

Plant a tree in the ground,
Plant a tree in your mind,
And speak with it about peace and calm,
Be a guardian of it,
Pray together for inner and outer peace.

Spend a time to know your beloved tree,
Celebrate this simple gift
And you will have a good friend,
To hug and intimately speak.

242

The talking Tree…
Blissful in the forest
Surrounded by fresh air
And blowing subtle and invisible breeze,
From the green fields
Like an angel of love,
Tree speaks and plea,
For inner and outer peace.

Tree has thousands of years,
A wide knowledge
And spontaneous wisdom,
A living creature of genuine humility,
Never running out of patience,
Tree is the eye of the way
For those who get lost and astray,
And the world collective lung
For fresh air to breathe.

Pastoral unity of being,
I talk to the green spirit
Of the trees,
Silently, in the woods,
In my mind,
In my vivid telepathic imagination
They talk through me
And send messages,
I smile and wave to them,

They smile back to me,
Signs they are happy to see me,
I sit down,
I watch and listen
And not interfere,
For the tree will certainly whispers and talks
With rustle of leaves,
And snap of wigs,
They are all individuals,
Just like people
And the rest on this earth.

Tree has no ear
But possesses a strong feeling,
That never fade away,
With a spirit that can listen
And efficiently communicate,
In a solitary contentment
And silent worshipping,
As a primitive form of belief,
Only Nature can make a tree,
If God could become a man
He can also become Tree,
Holy, Holy, Holy Lord Tree,
Wherever you may be,
Here and there
Let tree be our master!

243

Happy prison…
Tree does not move,
Silent is its life,
Redeemer from power of evil
In a state of romantic loneliness,
It is a bountiful beauty,
A source of inspiration and healing,
Time spent with a tree
Is never time wasted,
He who plants a tree loves others besides himself,
Tree good for health and wellbeing.

244

Wishing Tree…
I brought my troubles to a tree,
Escaping from suffering and loneliness
To reassure and pacify my mind,
I brought also a brightly coloured new ribbon,
I tied it on a wise Grandmother tree
Standing tall and strong,
Deeply rooted in loneliness in a green field,
Where the earth below
Is carpeted in green grass,
Hoping to elicit the spirit of the tree
To reach the state of beyond,
And declutter my mind
From many untidy things,
And I made a wish:
"*May Peace and Aboriginal Oneness*
Prevail on Earth and the I and not I,
Merrily reunite again."

245

Human face Tree…
Tree bearing flowers
Just like human face,
Without words and sounds
They just sweetly smile
And laugh too much,
Until its petals quietly and silently
Fall to the ground,
What a magic fairy tale,
In an enchanted forest.

246

Arcadia of Oneness…
Tree leads an idyllic existence,
It is high and mighty
In harmony with nature,
Fascinated by the patterns of the stars,
And the sweet sunshine
Of the blue sky.

Standing silently and patiently
On this land,
Opponent to shackle itself
Just let things completely at ease,
Wise like Mother Nature,
Tree does not hate,
Discriminate and judge,
But love all.
It is not absent of feeling,
With some unnameable attitude of mind
In which evil is accepted,
As though not condoned,
And makes friendship with it.
Tree is beyond good and bad,
A portal to another dimension.
What a pure kindness!

247

Loving tree more than man…
Walking, talking, hugging and listening
To trees with roots deep,
As beliefs everywhere
With the inner ear,
And giving them more and more care,
This is of the pleasures
In this fleeting world,
The heart inclined to the green trees.
Best friends for me,
Pillars of the world,
And spirits of nature
On the earth.
We never lose time and energy
Contemplating a tree,
My full name shall be:
"**Treeness Lover**"

Notes

The tree Arbol del Tule is one of the oldest trees in the world and is more than 2,000 years old. It is located on the church grounds in the town centre of Santa Maria del Tule in the Mexican state of Oaxaca. It was planted while Jesus Christ was alive.